In the Continuum

by Danai Gurira
and Nikkole Salter

A Samuel French Acting Edition

SAMUEL FRENCH

FOUNDED 1830

SAMUELFRENCH.COM

ISBN   978-0-573-65089-5   Printed in U.S.A.   #11715

MUSIC USE NOTE

Licensees are solely responsible for obtaining formal written permission from copyright owners to use copyrighted music in the performance of this play and are strongly cautioned to do so. If no such permission is obtained by the licensee, then the licensee must use only original music that the licensee owns and controls. Licensees are solely responsible and liable for all music clearances and shall indemnify the copyright owners of the play and their licensing agent, Samuel French, Inc., against any costs, expenses, losses and liabilities arising from the use of music by licensees.

IMPORTANT BILLING AND CREDIT
REQUIREMENTS

All producers of *IN THE CONTINUUM* *must* give credit to the Author of the Play in all programs distributed in connection with performances of the Play, and in all instances in which the title of the Play appears for the purposes of advertising, publicizing or otherwise exploiting the Play and/or a production. The name of the Author *must* appear on a separate line on which no other name appears, immediately following the title and *must* appear in size of type not less than fifty percent of the size of the title type.

IN THE CONTINUUM received its World Premiere in September 2005 at Primary Stages (Casey Childs, Executive Producer; Andrew Leynse, Artistic Director; Elliot Fox, Managing Director) in New York City. It subsequently moved to the Perry Street Theatre in November 2005, where it was produced by Primary Stages in association with Perry Street Theatre (David Elliott and Martin Platt, Co-Directors), Patrick Blake, Cheryl Wiesenfeld and Richard Jordan. The production was directed by Robert O'Hara, Associate Director was Gus Danowski with the following designers: Set, Peter R. Feuchtwanger; Costume, Sarah Hillard; Lighting, Colin D. Young; Sound, Lindsay Jones; Props, Jay Duckworth. Production Stage Managers were Kate Hefel and Samone B. Weissman with the followiong cast:

ABIGAIL and others	Danai Gurira
NIA and others	Nikkole Salter
Understudies	Tinashe Kajese and Antu Yacob

The original production toured from April 2006 through August 2007 to the following venues: Harare International Festival of the Arts, Harare, Zimbabwe; Baxter Theatre, Capetown, South Africa; Market Theatre, Johannesburg, South Africa; Traverse Theatre, Edinburgh, Scotland; Woolly Mammoth Theatre Company, Washington, DC; Cincinnati Playhouse, Cincinnati, OH; Center Theatre Group, Los Angeles, CA; Yale Repertory, New Haven, CT; Philadelphia Theatre Company, Philadelphia, PA; Goodman Theatre, Chicago, IL; and the Grahamstown National Arts Festival in South Africa.

IN THE CONTINUUM was work shopped at The Mud/Bone Theater in New York City, Michael Wiggins, Artistic Director, and developed in part at the Ojai Playwrights Conference, Robert Egan, Artistic Director.

HOW THIS PIECE IS PERFORMED

This piece was born of two actors deeply concerned about the experience of black women in the present fight against HIV/AIDS. Presently, with black women being the population with the highest rate of new infections both in the US and Africa – the co-creators of this piece (one African and one African American) felt the need to have a story told from the black woman's perspective; for her to be more than a statistic on a news report. This piece is designed for two actors to incorporate separate, yet parallel stories of an African and African American woman, and for both worlds to parallel and sometimes collide. Each character is real and is performed as such, not a commentary on a stereotype, but an illustration of three-dimensional human experiences in these societies. The piece as presently designed allows each actor to create their environments, both with sound and movement and minimal props. It is a minimalist piece, performed with no set, and only two chairs on stage. Lighting and sound elements can enhance the creation of each world but are used supportively and only when necessary – the actors create the environment with their bodies and voices. Though the piece is performed with mainly one character on stage at a time, there are moments where the worlds are shuffled in such a way that both the performers and worlds flow, overlap, juxtapose and cohabitate the stage throughout the performance. The stage directions are meant to clarify the way the piece is presently performed, but are by no means meant to restrict future incarnations of this piece.

PLACE

South Central, LA and Harare, Zimbabwe

*It is suggested that the play be performed with
no intermission.*

A NOTE FROM THE PLAYWRIGHTS

In the Continuum was born of our profound concern for the
experience of black women in the present fight against HIV/
AIDS. Black women currently represent the highest rate of
new infection both in the U.S. and Africa and this is a story
told from that perspective. Developed during our third year
of NYU's Graduate Acting Program with an invaluable artistic
community of students and teachers, it is a representation of
the humanity behind the statistics and an invitation for more
unheard stories to be brought "In(to) the Continuum."

PROLOGUE:
BACK IN THE DAY

(Children playing together – CHILD #1 in South Central, Los Angeles, CA; CHILD #2 in Harare, Zimbabwe.)

*CHILD #1. Come on! Com' on! I wanna play…I wanna play hopscotch! C'mon! Hopscotch! Just get some chalk! No, get a brick! Just bang it out. Then draw a circle. Yeah! *(Draws circle on the ground with a 'brick'.)* All the way around. I'ma show you how to play like this alright! But I'ma go first cuz I drew the circle. Huh? Okay, okay…One! Two! Three!

(She throws her marker in to the circle.)

*CHILD #2. Okay saka, totamba chi? Totamba nodo here? Ya! Saka une chalk here? Saka hauna? Oh, ndaiwona pano, mirai, – ngatigadzire circle rakadai, rakadai *(Draws circle on ground with chalk.)* Okay, ini ndotanga, one, two, three...

(Throws stone in the air, tries to catch it and it flies behind her.)

CHILD #2. Oh, shiiit.
CHILD #1. What?
*CHILD #2. Aiwa, richiri jana rangu, aiwa. No man, it's best of three! Iwe waka pusa! Ahh, saka hapana achatamba, hapana achatamba!

(She rubs out the chalk with her feet.)

 *CHILD #1. No! It's got to land in the middle of the circle. That's not the way you play the game. You stupid! Fine! *(She rubs out the chalk with her feet.)* Then nobody's playin' this game then! Ain't nobody playin'!

 BOTH CHILDREN.
(Singing & dancing together.)
TOMATO SAUCE, SAUCE,
SAUCE, SAUCE, SAUCE, SAUCE (2X)
ELIZABETH, ABETH,
ABE, BE, BE, BETH (2X)
CHIPIKINRINGO, GO
GO, GO, GO, GO (2X)

COUSIN'S ON THE CORNER IN THE WELFARE LINE
BROTHER'S IN THE SLAMMER, HE COMMITTED A
  CRIME
PREACHER'S IN THE CLUB ON THE DOWN LOW
  CREEP
AND YO' MAMA'S IN THE GUTTER SCREAMIN' H-I-V

(The children separate into their distinct worlds, no longer playing together.)

 *CHILD #1. What you say about my mama?
 *CHILD #2. Saka wati amai vangu vari HIV?
 *CHILD #1. Yo' mama got HIV.
 *CHILD #2. Amai vako ndivo vari HIV.
 *CHILD #1. Yo' mama, yo' daddy, yo' whole generation

got HIV!

*CHILD #2. Amai vako, nababa vako, nevese vemumhuri menyu vari HIV.

*CHILD #1. You stupid! And you got HIV! And yo' mama got a cauliflower growin' out of her pussy!

*CHILD #2. Iwe waka pusa, newewo uri HIV; futi Amai vako vane maronda panaapa.

BOTH CHILDREN. Ewww!

ONE: IN THE BEGINNING

(The two actresses continue separate conversations in their separate worlds as ABIGAIL and NIA. ABIGAIL takes a seat and commences reading a news report at Zimbabwe Broadcasting Corporation Studios. NIA is in a stall of a bathroom in a hip-hop night club, hovering over the toilet.)

ABIGAIL. Good evening and welcome to the 8 o'clock main news bulletin. I am Abigail Murambe. Harare. The minister of agriculture comrade Nixton Chibanda warned against any reports by the biased and slandering Western Media which assert that Zimbabwe is facing a famine. He further commented that these irresponsible journalists and their evil cohorts have been the source of Zimbabwe's expulsion from the Commonwealth as well as the crippling sanctions imposed by the United Nations. He asserted that contrary to such reports, Zimbabwe will in fact produce a surplus of agricultural crops in the coming harvest. He admonished against nastyers who...Ahh, ahh, what is nastyers? Naysayers? Whooa, ah, but it says nastyers ka. And what is naysayers, someone who says nay? Ah, hey, are we in Shakespeare or what. Okay, why can't they just say liars or something? Ahh, ahh, look at all these typos man!! And since when was the vice president's name Janet Mujuru? Its Joyce Mujuru man, you want to get me fired?

NIA. *(She vomits.)* It feel like I'm dying. No, I'll be okay. Just give me a second. I haven't had nothin' to eat — I keep throwin' everything up. Nasty cafeteria food. All I had was a Long Island Iced tea. I know I should eat something. Just give me a second. I'll get it myself. I don't know, Trina. It mighta been in the weed — I ain't the weed expert. They was passin' it, it was free, I took just some. *(ABIGAIL sits at mirror — touches up makeup with tissue.)* I think it's somethin' else. Cuz nothin' taste the same, don't nothin' smell the same — I ain't old! Just cuz you popped outta yo' mama coochie yesterday don't make me *(Starts to throw up.)* — Trina, just pass me some tissue!

ABIGAIL. Ewe, wait, is there any shine here? Okay *(Dabs side of face, drops tissue to the floor, NIA picks it up.)*. Thanks. And, can I have the rest of the report please?! *(Perusing report.)* Hey, it's getting harder and harder to even say this crap man. I can't believe — Huh? No I wasn't saying anything. But, Evermore, have you gotten your pay check? Ah, NO I haven't, its been six weeks now, how am I supposed to pay school fees with air? Right now I am near penniless. This is what we get for working for the government, ini I want to move into the private sector, South Africa man! SABC! Real money, shamwari! Ah, I am just as good as them, probably better! Then from there CNN!!! Why not, I bet I am just as good as them, probably better. *(NIA flushes the toilet and exits the stall.)* Where is my tea by the way, Evermore, can you please, please bring me my tea BEFORE we start, I need to calm my nerves. Four sugars.

(ABIGAIL sits — jots notes on her tasks for the day on news report.)

NIA. My breath smell like raw fish and old tacos. No, I don't wanna go. *(Looking into an imagined full-length mirror.)* I got all dressed up so I could celebrate with Darnell, so that's what I'ma do. 'Cause, I don't see him everyday no more, so when he get here I wanna look good. *(Fixing her hair.)* No, he just be out, doin' his college thang, but in two more days, all this scholarship stuff will be done. We been together ten months and three weeks, I can wait two more days. Huh? Yep, it's almost been a year. He practically my husband. *(Fishing out lipgloss.)* 'Cause we been through so much! Like last summer, when he got jumped by them Piru niggas; girl, I was so scared! But I was the first one to visit when he got home. And when everything went down with my mom's I would run away from the foster homes and Darnell would let me sneak and stay with him 'til I got my spot at Good Shepard. And if that ain't love, — He even came to see when I won that poetry contest. *(Applying lipgloss.)* Girl, yes! They gave us a big banquet; I got $500 — and a plaque. And the judges said I was — what they call it? — "full of potential". I know, I didn't have no potential before, but now that I can talk they poetry language, I'm "full of potential". *(Closing lipgloss.)* It ain't hard, all they have you do is follow a pattern and write it out — A pattern! — Okay, like: *(Using the lipgloss to count the syllables on her fingers.)* Bright ass sun-ny day – 5 syllables. Burn-in' the shit out-ta me – 7. I wish it was cold – 5. See. No, I think about them all the time. It just come to me. It's easy. It's just like flowin'. Try one. Just try one. Alright, I'ma start you, okay? Okay. Dir-ty ass, skank…humm? — *(Waiting for TRINA to fill in the blank.)* Hoe! Good! Wit yo' crun-chy hair — *(To TRINA.)* wit yo' fake weave? — no, no, wait I got it. Wit yo' crun-chy ba-by hair - 7. Leave Dar-nell a-lone -5.

(Begins fishing mascara out of her purse.)

ABIGAIL. By the way, before I forget, I next time I want to be dressed by Truworths — because Edgars keeps bringing these clothes that make me look like I have grandchildren or something. Thank you for that Evermore, I know I am a married woman, that doesn't mean I have to look like I am selling vegetables paroadside. Next time they bring such things I am just going to say no, they must know I am their model, saka they're supposed to make me look good.

NIA. *(Applying mascara.)* Shut up, Trina! I always look good. Please! I look better than those groupies! Did you see that girl that had on the — So. *(Putting mascara away.)* So what! So, Darnell looks at them, so what! Girls walking around with they titties hangin' out tryin'ta get looked at. *(Fixing her clothes.)* He might look at them but he goin' home with me. Don't worry, tonight, I'ma just let him celebrate. But Saturday night, after his scholarship ceremony, *(Imitating female video dancers in hip-hop music videos.)* I'ma give him somethin' to look at. *(She laughs.)* Huh? What, my new purse? Yeah, it was a gift — courtesy of Nordstrom. *(Fishing for and applying perfume purse.)* Girl, please. A playa like me don't pay fo' nothin'. *(Pretending to steal the purse.)* Everything I got on was a five finger discount. Wait! No! Cuz the way I see it, it only cost fifty cents for these companies to make; they only pay Javier and them ten cent to put it together; they pay me five wack ass dollars an hour, then they go sell it for a hundred and fifty? Do I look like a dummy? Please, me takin' this purse is part of my community service. I wish I would pay a hundred and fifty!

ABIGAIL. Mmm, mmm, Evermore, forget about that tea. I am not feeling well. Ahh, we better do this thing quickly guys. Where's the cameraman? Oh oh oh, is Gibson not here yet? Finish. But shame — he told me he has no transport, hanzi he has to wake up at 3 am to reach here by 7! *(NIA returns to the bathroom stall.)* Ahh, times are hard suwa. MunomuZimbabwe sha. Oh, is he still feeling sick? He wasn't looking very well. Shame...But Evermore, you are looking plumper these days, where are you finding sadza munomuZimbabwe? Please can you direct us all there? No, no tea please, I'm not feeling well...

NIA. I never get sick. No, never! When have you seen me — ? I don't be sick for real at school. No! I be fakin'! Yeah. I guess I'ma good actress — liar, actress, whatever. Like you ain't never lied about havin' cramps to get outta sex ed. Shoot, when I realized that worked, I would be havin' my period like two, three times a month. I mean, it's not like they gon' check! What they gonna do, look? — Oooh! Hay! Shh! Be quiet. You hear that?

ABIGAIL. Ahh, I think I hear Gibson out there.

NIA. That's my jam. Me and Darnell always dance to that. They would play our song when I'm on the toilet.

*ABIGAIL. *(Gets up.)* Yes Gibson, muri right? / Are you feeling better — good good. / Evermore checkai for lint! / Let's go. *(Looking in the mirror.)* / Yes I am ready! / Wait where is my special ballpoint?! / *(Finds it in her hand.)* Oh, it's right here. / Totanga ka! / Let's go!

*NIA. Trina...? / Trina, why you so quiet? / You takin' a dump? / You don't take a dump in a public bathroom! / You nasty! / *(Looking in the mirror.)* Yeah, I guess I feel a little better. / Do me a favor: go get me a breath mint or somethin. / Hurry up!

(Gunshots. NIA runs out.)

BLACKOUT in BOTH WORLDS

ABIGAIL. Oh, no tell me your joking, another powercut!! This is the third one today! We won't be finished till night time! Twenty minutes? Okay please, ndapota. AND can we get some sort of lights here please! *(Sits back down.)* Better be twenty minutes, last time it was three hours. Ha, its bad enough we had to work so late all last week, you know ma in-laws they start to say marara — "hey hey that is why she only has one child" — imagine! "We want more children here, Simbi is getting lonely! You mustn't work so much!" This coming from inlaws who have never given me a bubble gum or a fork at my wedding. But, *(Looks around.)* they can shut up now Evermore, baby number 2 is on the way!! Ya! Pururudza! Tofara tese! Hmmm? I just found out on Monday! Stamford doesn't even know yet, I am going to tell him and that family of his at Simbi's birthday party on Sunday. Ya, he's turning seven, he's a big boy now - time for another, one that looks like the mother. Simbi? He looks just like his father man, with that big nose — shame. Stanford? He's fine...he just keeps doing too much of those late nights I told you about — I don't like it man! These men, they want to play away and have us at home at the same time — he's got to stop that. But, you know, I think another baby will make him act better; Auntie always said showing the husband you are a good and fertile wife will keep him indoors.

Oh, by the way Evermore — you chased your man out when you caught him with the other woman? Ah, no, that's not the answer man — no its not, because then that other woman, hure that she is, will get everything you have been working for! Ah no me, I realized the solution: men are like bulls searching for pastureland, you show them greener grass and they stay put, and this baby is greener grass. He's going to stay put now. Hey, Stanford, he wants to forget how hard he had to work for me! ME? I was known as the Ice Queen! Hmmmhmm! No one could get near me — I was very, very picky. I used to go to those house parties and I was the best dancer — EH HE, suwa, *(Gets up, begins to dance.)* Wonai, wonai — ha, I've still got it! Ah, Evermore! Do you remember this one? This one? It was big around '92, '93 — I hated it but it was so popular I had to know how to do it — WELL. Do you remember what it was called — ABORTION!! Imagine! So nasty hey! And the men wanted to come from behind! Ha, no me I would say "Just look hey, don't touch!" But then along came Stamford Murambe — ah, with him I was like *(Bending over.)*, "You can touch, please touch!" *(Laughing)*Ya, ya he won me over, fair and square, but he had to persevere! With maletters, flowers! Me I didn't come easy ka! *(Sits back down.)*. He wants to forget all of that. He'll come around, he just needs another boy. A girl?! What am I going to do with a girl in this world? No, two boys that's perfect. And they're going to grow up in Chisipiti or Glen Lorne, — no we can't stay in Hatfield anymore, ahh, it's too filled with strong rural types, too many muboi! I am sick and tired of living next door to people who keep chickens and goats in their backyard, I want to be around the poshy!! Those who know how to eat with a knife and fork. And our new house will have a swimming pool, DSTV, maybe a tennis court. Stamford can drive the

Pajero because I'll drive the benz. And the kids will go to St John's prep or Hartman House and learn the best these whites can teach, and I have a good feeling about this one *(Points at stomach.)* he could become the next Kofi Anan, or Bill Gates — why not! And Stamford will love this one so much; hmmhmm, he will take one look at him and never forget where home is again. *(Phone rings.)* Oh, that's mine! I thought I turn it off! Oh, let me take this Evermore it's the clinic...Hello.....yes…this is Mrs Abigail Murambe… *(Exiting.)*

TWO: NIA'S DREAM

NIA. *(Looking behind emergency room curtains.)* Trina…? Trina…oh, sorry! *(Sucking her teeth.)* My bad. Trina? Hey. *(Entering into TRINA'S space.)* How you doin'? Good. Did you do what I told you? Lemme see your wrist — Why not? I said don't give them your real information! You did give them your real name! You such a scaredy cat. What they gon' do, spank you? Cuz! Now they gonna call Good Shepherd and then everybody gon' be all up in our business. Has the doctor even come in here yet? Be right back? Please, if we was dyin' we'd already be dead. Lemme see it. *(She looks at TRINA'S wound.)* At least it not bleedin' no more. *(Sitting)* Me? I think I got to get some stitches. Yeah. No, wait, the doctor was like, 'How did you get glass stuck in your side?" I was like, "Duh! They was shootin', people was goin' crazy! You get knocked over and stomped on you while you lyin' on a floor full-a shot-up glass and see what happen to you!" Yeah, you laughin' now, *(Beat)* but you looked fucked up then. I ain't gon' lie — all I saw was blood, you know, and I got scared. I was like, *(Like an exaggerated mother crying over a child's coffin a la BOYZ IN THE HOOD.)* Oh,

Lawd! *(In a Baptist Church breakdown.)* Don't let Trina die! Please don't let Trina die!!! Lawd no! *(Laughing)* You shhh! *You* silly! Okay, lemme see it again. At least it's gonna make a cute scar. I'm just glad you okay. Nothin'. Okay. But if I tell you somethin' Trina, you promise not to go tellin' everybody? Okay. No, the doctor wanted to give me this x-ray to see if I like broke a rib or somethin', but she made me pee in this cup to see if I was pregnant first, and…I am. I know I'ma get kicked out. I don't know what — She just gave me all these pamphlets, and did all these tests. Now I'm supposed to come back tomorrow but — Of course, I'm gonna tell Darnell! Yes, I am! I'ma go right up to his practice…and I'm gonna take his hand and put it on my stomach, look up at him and say, "Darnell, I'm pregnant." And he gon' look down at me and say, "For real?" and I'ma say, "ummm, humm." *(Laughing)* Then, he gon' get on his knees and put his ear against my belly and listen. Umm, humm! And then he gon' look up at me and say, "My son in there?" and I'ma say, "umm-humm." Then, we're gonna get married. Umm-humm. And move into a big-ass house cuz he gon' play for the Lakers and I'll just be — Oooh, shut up! Oh, I'll be rich doin' somethin'. Watch! *(Getting her cell phone out of her purse.)* I'll call him right now. I will tell him! Just watch and learn. *(She dials.)* Voicemail? 'Darnell! Where are you? It's Nia. We was at the club waitin' for you — you will not believe what happened. I'll tell you all about it when you come pick us up — me and Trina at the hospital. We need a ride. And, uh…*(To TRINA.)* Shut up, I am! *(Into the phone again.)* I…I got somethin' to tell you. Just call me back. No! Why haven't *you* called me? That's what's more important! It's been like four hours — !

THREE: THE DIAGNOSIS

NURSE MUGOBO. *(Steps out banging clip board.)* Please, this is a clinic.

NIA. *(As if the nurse has chastised her for her cell phone usage.)* My bad. I just —

NURSE. Please, Can you control your children, they can't run around like eh…monkeys!

NIA. I'm comin' back! Dag! I got to go, this lady trippin' talkin' 'bout I can't be on my cell phone. Call me when you get this message. I love you. *(Putting away her cell phone.)*

NURSE. *(Looks at clipboard, talking to ABIGAIL.)* Right, Mrs Choto? You are not Mrs Choto. Mrs Choto, Mrs Choto!!!!

NIA. That is my real name. Why would I — Can I go!

NURSE. Ha, and vanhu vatema vanonetsa. *(Flips to next chart.)* Mrs Murindi? Murambe, ya, sorry, Abigail? Right. *(Looks through chart.)* I have your chart here...

NIA: My chart? Ya'll gon' call — ? *(Sucking her teeth.)*

NURSE. Everything looks fi- oh.

NIA. What?

NURSE. You have tested HIV positive. This means you have the virus that causes the Acquired Immune Deficiency syndrome…

NIA. I'm sorry what?

NURSE. ...there is no cure for Aids, it is generally transmitted through unprotected penetrative sex, anal or vaginal //with a person infected with HIV. And unprotected sex means sex without a condom, male or female to protect the sexual organs and in Africa that is generally through heterosexual contact.

NIA. //You trying say I'ma hoe? Do I look like a junkie?

Do it look like I'm gay? Do I look like I'm from Africa? No! Every time we come in here ya'll try to make us feel like we're dirty or stupid or something. *(Pulling out her cell phone.)* You don't know what the fuck you're talkin' about — s'cuse you — no, S'CUSE YOU! *(She EXITS.)*

NURSE. We therefore recommend that from now on *(Eyes follow NIA – to passing orderly.)* Ewe what are you doing? Yes I can see that — but can't you see those are dripping on the floor? Take them to the back, those are contaminated. Yes they are! You barance wemunhu. *(Eyes follow him out. Back to ABIGAIL.)* We therefore strongly recommend your practice abstinence from now on; but if you must, please can you protect others, there are three condoms, sorry we have run out. If you want we can show you how to use them on a banana in the next room. *(Eyes wander.)* But then you will only have two. Excuse me. Eh, Sisi Getty, are you going to the shops? Please Sisi help me sha, I am so hungry can you just buy me a sweet bun ne a coke? Thank you Sisi. Aiwa, I have the money, mirai. *(Looks over at ABIGAIL.)* Ah Miss, Miss — *(Looks at chart.)* Miss Abigail, why are you crying? No, aiwa, you must think clearly mange. I see here you have a son? Bring him in, we can test him also. *(Finds no money in bra.)* Ahh, sorry Sisi I forgot my money — Oh…thank you Sisi you are a life saver — surely, every time! *(Looks after SISI GETTY smiling, returns to ABIGAIL, smile fades.)* Right, so, we must see your husband in the next few days — he must be formally informed and tested. Ah, AH Miss, Miss Abigail — there are no exceptions for that — I know it can be dangerous to tell him, many women are scared he will beat them and take the children — what, what, even though usually its coming from him, but, sorry you tested first. SO — you must tell him and bring him for testing. Even with the risky business of it. And we must see him as soon as possible, nhasi riri Friday saka on Monday, latest; we can make the appointment right now. *(Looks down at chart.)* Ah, *(Stops, puts down pen.)* you are pregnant? Ah…you women. You go and get this HIV then you want to have a baby or two? It's not good, munoziwa, its not good. *(Goes back to chart.).* Drugs? Ah we don't have them here, if you have money you can try to find them, they are very, very expensive. Otherwise, change your diet — eat greens, negrains, nemeat. And don't breastfeed. We will test the baby soon after it is born. So we will see you and Mr Stamford Mirindi, sorry Murambe, on Monday, 10am. Please amai, if you don't come I will be forced to call him. Right. *(Flips to next chart.)* Mrs Choto, Mrs Cho — *(NIA rushes in — referring to her as though she is MRS CHOTO.)* there you are, you are late, can you sit down. Ha, and vanhu vatema vanonetsa.

FOUR: NIA'S DENIAL

NIA. Trina, get your stuff. Let's go. Just get your stuff! I called Patti, she gon' give us a ride, but leavin' right — Yes, I called Probation Patti — to get us a ride, Trina. Who else was I gonna call? My mama? What for? She don't care about me. Why don't you call yo' mama? — forget Darnell. He not comin'— Whatchu yellin' at me for? How is any of this my fault? You the one said you could hang. You the one begged me to come — If you didn't go — get yourself shot we wouldn't have this problem. Did I stutter? You was the only idiot walkin' around when people shootin'. Ain't you ever heard gunshots before? You supposta get down. Duck, stupid! *You* messed everything up! We was supposed to sneak out, go to the Club, have some fun, sneak back in — nobody was gon' know. Now I gotta listen to Patti's bougie mouth, all for what? Yo' bullet scratch and a couple-a stitches that you won't even see after two months with some cocoa butter!? I'm the one brought you here and made sure you got taken care of. I shoulda left yo' stank ass there. And just went back by myself. Then I wouldn't be here. I ain't even supposed to be here — ! Nothin's wrong!

I'm pregnant stupid. Whatchu think?

I don't see what you so worried about, Trina. All they gon' tell you is not to sneak out no more. I'm the one who can't go back to Good Shepard. If anybody should be mad, it should be me. And I figured Patti was gon' find out anyway cuz you used your real name — So if we gon' get caught, we might as well have a ride! Just get your stuff. Let's go.

FIVE: HAVE MERCY
(ABIGAIL on the street, trying to flag down a ride.)

ABIGAIL. *(To street kids.)* Fotsek! You kids get away. NO I don't have any money. Don't touch me! I'll beat you like your mother should have. *(Pause).* Just go away. Please *(Phone rings. ABIGAIL starts, petrified, she pulls the phone out of her purse.)* Hello Stamfo —. Simbi *(Laughs, cries — relieved.).* Hello my big boy. How are you — no mummy is just happy to hear from you that's all — but what did mama say to you about calling her cell phone from the landline? NO, I said it's very expensive so you mustn't. What's wrong my beby, why are you calling me? Is daddy home? No don't put him on. No no, no, no, mummy doesn't' need to speak to him right now, just don't

put him on. Don't. Okay. *(Trying to flag down omnibus taxi.)*
No, I am catching a commuter omnibus, so let mummy go so
that I can catch one okay. *(To street kids.)* Ewe fotsek, I said I
don't have any money. No, no not you baby. What? What did
you put in my handbag? Simbi, I don't have time for this —
okay, okay, okay *(Finds folded paper in handbag.)* what is this
Simbi? This is beautiful, did you draw it yourself? Okay, So
who is the first person? Quickly, quickly. That's deddy, okay.
And who is this one in the middle?! That's mummy? Okay!
And who is the last one? That's you? Simbi you are funny!
Why are you bigger than everyone else Simbi? But Simbi this
is beautiful, we will to put it on the fridge when I get home. But
Simbi, next time you draw mummy don't draw her with hair
that's going all over the place like that! Mummy's hair doesn't
do that beby. Just draw me with simple hair, one, two, three,
four, five neat little strokes that's all. But beby this is beautiful.
(To pestering street kids.) Fotsek, go away, you kids, where are
your parents…*(Slowly turns back around to streetkids.)* Fotsek,
go away, please, get away, just go. *(Flagging down ride.)* Simbi,
Mama has to go now, okay, now you go to eat; see I just stopped
one, I have to go. Mommy's coming.

SIX: CHATTER HEADS

PATTI. Gosh! I cannot believe, at the peak of rush hour I
had to — Nia!
PETRONELLA. *(More British than the British.)* Abigail!
PATTI. Not you Trina, you wait inside!
PETRONELLA. Abigail Moyo!
PATTI. Nia, you get in!

PETRONELLA. Get in, get in! It's me, Petronella Siyanyarambazinyika!

PATTI. *(To driver.)* The 105 *(One o five.)* to the 110 *(One ten.)* 405 *(Four o five.)* to Beach Avenue and Centinela, please. Yeah.

PETRONELLA. How are you my dear??? I haven't seen you since — is it high school? Oh, my gosh its been too long! AH, but your looking well, kept that figure. Just tell Lovemore where you want to go. The city centre? Is that safe Lovemore? Okay. Good.

PATTI. I am not angry, Nia. Did you think I was angry? 'Cause I'm not. I'm dumfounded, I'm worried, I'm completely devastated! We've been through Independent Living Classes, Life Skills Assessment, Job Readiness Training — we were getting somewhere, Nia! What was so important at this club that it was worth giving up everything we've worked for? And I tell you, if I miss my flight to Milwaukee for the second part of the Journey toward Self Discovery Conference I'll —

PETRONELLA. And did I hear correctly that you married Stamford Murambe? HAA, well done my dear, he was gorgeous!! What a bloody catch! Oh, you still have him right? Whew! But good work my dear everyone wanted a piece of him!!! I too have officially joined the married club! Mmmhmm, just two years ago, do you remember Farai Mungoshi? Prince Edward, headboy, captain of the rugby team, a real feast for the eyes? No, I married his younger brother Richard.

PATTI. …Yes, but you tell the universe exactly what you want to experience by the choices you make every moment. And I know we don't always make the best choices, but — Yes, even me, I don't always — Okay. Like yesterday, I was having lunch in the cafeteria and I had not one, but two helpings of macaroni and cheese. Not the best choice, no, but not going to drastically change my life. You take the good job I found you at Nordstrom and chose to get fired by stealing — again. I've given you the easiest course curriculum developed for continuing education yet you throw away your chance at a diploma by ditching. You take the free housing in Westwood I gave you, and was asked to leave because you wouldn't keep curfew. I've even violated the state's abstinence only policy and given you condoms! Now you're telling me that one night of hangin' wit the homies, rockin' your phat gear and sportin' your big chain with the medallion of the mother land and shakin' your booty with some boy at some club is worth getting shot at? *(Beat)* Okay. Good answer. So: With my choices, I'm telling the universe that I…want….to be fat. But, so what, big deal, we're talking about you!. You're telling the universe that you want to be an uneducated, unemployed, homeless, kleptomaniac, soul train dancer. Is that what you want? If you were in my shoes, what would you do?

PETRONELLA. … oh you got those here? They look just look just like my Stella McCartney pumps. I know her personally actually, she gave me a pair — she couldn't give them to her step mum — she's only got one leg! Did you say you worked ZBC? Oh, *(Laughs)* no, I am sorry, I just got back home so I am still adjusting to all the lingo, and someone the other day called it Dead BC. Good for you though hey! You were always a great public speaker! Me, oh, well...I went abroad soon after high school, to study at London School of Economics, I was there for both my undergrad and my masters, International Relations with a focus on Human Rights and Gender Development, and I am still there mostly, I work as a consultant for big organizations, the UN, OXFAM, stuff like that. Right now, I have been really focused on HIV and Southern African women and of course all the big organizations abroad are going to hire me right? I am like this perfect poster child — but I can't complain, I've been working with DATA — oh come on you know — Debt, AIDS, Trade, Africa — Bono — he's a rock star — he has an organization. *(Car swerves.)* Careful Lovemore!

PATTI. Ah, pardon, sir —

PETRONELLA. God, the way people drive in this country!

PATTI. Yes, but that clearly said, 'no left turn' —

PETRONELLA. In England he would have been arrested on the spot!

PATTI. It is illegal! — I should write down your number and report — It's just that it's a very risky turn, sir, and we have precious cargo. Yeah! Thanks. *(To NIA.)* Perfect example: There are many ways to get to Inglewood, but making an illegal short cut turn here is not one of them. There are no shortcuts in life, Nia! The laws are designed to keep us safe. And I hate to burst your bubble, but, no matter where you go there will be rules. On this road there are rules, gangs have rules, even in the wilderness there are rules. And there are consequences in choosing to violate the rules. Are you listening to me? Nia!

PETRONELLA. ...there's not even any bloody petrol! This is not the country we grew up in. How do you survive? Anyway, concerning the whole AIDS issue — I was actually trying to get some statistics — that's why I was at the clinic — naturally the head nurse was on a two hour lunch or something! Zimboes! And of course you have to get the highest statistics possible in order to get them to do anything. That's when they get all aghast and say, 'Oh those poor Africans who can't help themselves — let's bring them our great answers' — which are WHAT?

Okay — they are manufacturing some drugs here, but believe me they aren't the best kind and how is anyone supposed to be able to afford them long term in this economy? It's a bloody mess! And you want to know why? You want to know why? I'll tell you why. It's because we've been programmed. Yes! Because we look to them as our source of hope and redemption. Meanwhile we have the answers and we don't know it. I have been thinking a lot about our own traditional AFRICAN healing and I — No! I am not saying have the cure or whatever, but there is something in it, you can't argue that. Do you remember Sisi Thembi?

PATTI. ...the value is not in material things. Nia, I don't know what I can give you that's more important than the opportunity to lift yourself up. That's what I did. Yeah. It may not look like it, but I'm from the 'hood — well, Ladera Heights — but I drove down Crenshaw every day — It doesn't matter! It doesn't matter your race or your gender or where you're from, it's where you're going. But I think you want to stay in the ghetto because no matter what I show you, no matter where I put you, you carry it with you in your mind. Now, you can either take that Emergency Services number, call, and stay in a shelter tonight; or you can pick yourself up, march yourself in there and patch things up with your mother. A girl needs her mother, Nia. You know, my mother and I never got along either — well...it's 'cause she never really cultivated my garden of talents, it was either her way or no way, and I know you and your mother are experiencing a rift, that's the connection — okay, okay! I know, I know! I'm all in the "kool-aid" —

PETRONELLA. ...remember when we caught her talking to trees?

PATTI. — my bad...

PETRONELLA. And she used to roast grasshoppers!
PATTI. …I learned that yesterday. //Did I say it right?
BOTH. //hahahahahhahahahahahaha…..hheee….heee..
PATTI. Nia?
PETRONELLA. Abi?
PATTI. Are you alright? Okay.

You know, I was online yesterday, surfing the web, and I saw that the city is looking for poetry to display on the new eco-efficient trains. I think you're work is perfect. Go online, download an application and submit some of your work. If you win, it's more scholarship money for when you — when you decide to go to community college. And your poems won at the Success is Our Future Ceremony, now that's something! Believe you me there are plenty of opportunities out there for a girl like you!! You can still be anything you want to be!!! *(Light bulb.)* Change the course of history. Don't let yesterday's bad choices keep you from making good choices today. Huh!?! But I know you. I can tell, you're gonna do the right thing! Hey, there's no place for you to go but up, HUH!!?? – Huh? Well, you could go down and spiral…

PETRONELLA. …she was such a mad, mad, MAD, woman — Sisi Thembi! I can't believe she is in the church now! Like every day that sort of thing? Oh what a shame, hey — remember how she swore by witchdoctors? Remember how her…daughter, her daughter — had some sickness no one could figure out – she said her witchdoctor — sorry — traditional healer-fixed it! She had to do some strange things but it worked and nothing else did. There is something to it I tell you. What? You want to get out here? Abi there is nothing — ABIGAIL — What are you doing the car is still moving. Lovemore stop the car! *(Getting out of car, yelling.)*

PATTI. Bye, Nia!

PETRONELLA. Abigail, wait!!!!

PATTI. *(Getting out of car, yelling.)* Nia, wait!

PETRONELLA. You work for ZBC — do you host that show Breaking New Ground?

PATTI. Tell you mother I said hello!

PETRONELLA. No…well I really want to be on it, I think I have a lot to say this the country needs to hear, I am breaking new bloody ground…

PATTI. I'm an Audi.

PETRONELLA. How do you say "bye" again Lovemore? Oh — CHISARAI!!!

PATTI. Five Thousand!

PETRONELLA. NO, what's the other one — TICH-AMBOONA!!!

PATTI. No, Audi, like the car, but 'out of here'! *(Makes the sound of a car speeding by.)* Nevermind…just go, go, go...

(Her laughing at herself turns into…)

SEVEN: MAMA

(Friday morning. MAMA'S porch. She's calming her crying baby throughout the scene.)

MAMA. *(*IMANI, a six-month old baby, crying. Sound is made by actress.)* *Hey! Hey!! Get offa my grass! Get offa my grass and take your Funyion bag with you. *(To herself.)* Bad ass kids. *(Beat)* * Well, well, well. I knew you'd come back. Lemme guess: They didn't believe your lies at the Good Shepard either, huh? You thought it was gon' be easy as that. Well, life is not easy, guess you got to learn the hard way. And now you wanna come back. I'm still goin' to family court off of the shit you pulled; anger management, freakin' parenting classes like I don't know what the hell I'm doin', and you wanna come back just like that? No apology, no nothin'? And then you got the nerve to ask me for $400! I tell you — how you gon' pay me back? You got a job? You lookin' like a damn prostitute, what are you wearin'? It's nine o'clock in the morning, walkin' 'round like you been walkin' the streets. *(Baby talk to IMANI.)* She walkin' the streets, ain't she? Ain't she? *(Seriously)* Is you walkin' the streets, Nia? Don't get smart with me! Then what you need $400 for, huh? Probably some Guess jeans. What happened to the money from that poetry contest? Ain't nobody payin' you to put'ch'a little rhymes together no more? Ain't got no job, no place to live, but spend all yo' time writin' poetry and shoppin' — for $400 Guess jeans. Are they self-cleaning? Do they pay rent? If anybody's getting $400 'round here, 'guess' who it's gonna be — ME. I'm tired of comin' second to ya'll. I can't remember the last time I had me some lotion or some new panties. Besides, you grown, remember? And us grown folk, we pay for our own shit. You old enough. Hell, when I was 19 I was * — And don't think you slick goin' behind my back askin' Marvin for the money. I thought you didn't like him. He ain'tchya daddy, so stop askin' him fo' shit. *(To IMANI.)* Huh? He's yo' daddy, huh? Yo' daddy! Who's yo' daddy? That's yo' daddy! *(To NIA.)* I don't know. You should ask that lil' boyfriend of yours, Darnell, for $400. He'll buy them pants for you...since he the one like to get in 'em so often. Don't think I didn't usta hear your little narrow behind climbin' out the window to go oochie coochie with that boy. Like you the first one discovered how to sneak out the house? I invented that shit. I already been everywhere you been, Nia. I was just tryin' to keep your fast ass from goin' to half of them places. OH! But you 'grown'! Well, I'ma tell yo' grown ass this: I know you like him, and he look like he goin' places,* but don't you end up pregnant, Nia. Cuz once you turn this switch on, you can't turn it off, and I'ma be damned if I end up raisin' your kids cuz you couldn't use a condom. Oh, OH! *(To IMANI.)* She woman enough to do the do, but she can't talk the talk. *(To NIA.)* What would you rather I say, Ms. Nia? Look at me. Strap on the jimmy? Pull the balloon over the sausage? I wish somebody had told me about this shit, half-a ya'll wouldn't be here. And now days, you can catch all kinda stuff. Stuff you can't get rid of cuz it gets in your blood. Trust me: three minutes of slappin' bellies ain't worth death. And that's what it is, death. * Because it's a government experiment, it was designed — They've done it before and will do it again. You think it's consequential that we the ones got it the most out of everybody. They been tryin' to get rid of us since the Emancipation Proclamation. First they lynched us, then they got us high so they could put us in prison. Then they got the ones that ain't incarcerated to shoot up each other and now they brought this hopin' that we fuck ourselves to death. And you know they got a cure. What you think the whole civilian rights was about? That's why they really assassinated Martin: to distract us from the monkey fuckers that brought it back from Africa to kill us. And they killed Malcolm cuz, on his pilgrimage, he found out who the monkey fuckers were. You got to know your history. That's what's wrong with ya'll — I know, I know, you love Darnell. Darnell love you. Ya'll invincible in love. Yes, I know. I was in love too, okay. Five times. Remember that. All I had to worry about was getting' pregnant, but ya'll got a whole slew of other stuff you got to think about. Real love lasts forever, but so do real mistakes. *(To IMANI.)* Yes, they do, huh? Yes they do! And I'ma tell you, just like I tol' them, yes I am, yes I am! You only got me 'til you're 18. That's it! Count down!* *(To NIA.)* That's it. Now you can go on in the back and get $60 outta my purse so that you can get you a room to rent for the night, cuz you can't stay here. I ain't gonna let ya'll run my world forever. And, uh, you grown, remember? And I ain't gonna let you scare this man away. Shiiit. One down four to go. Look at them. That's exactly what I'm — Hey! HEY! Well, stop sprayin' paint on them walls, that shit ain't art!* *(She EXITS.)*

EIGHT: THE CHURCH

("Akuna wakaita saJesu" is being sung by the congregation, ABIGAIL rushes in, trying to look normal, greets people and sing and dances along as she searches for SISITHEMBI.)

ABIGAIL. *(Singing along.)* Hallo auntie! Muri right? Ya, Stamford is fine thanks! Hi Pastor Manyika! How are you? No, we have had trouble with transport, no petrol ka! Otherwise twice a week I would come to worship!! Shit *(Sees SISITHEMBI.)* Sisi Thembi — SisiThembi wuya! Ahh *(Makes her way through the pews.)* Excuse me, sorry, pamsoroi! Sorry baby, don't cry. Excuse me please…thanks *(Manoevers around a rather large man. Reaches SISITHEMBI tries to sing, and look natural.)* SisiThembi, I need the address of the, eh, *(Looks up at large man.)* remember that man you said helped you when your daughter was sick? NOO! The man with the eh, eh — herbs — Come on. Okay look at me — the — *(Imitates a witchdoctor possessed.).* THE WITCHDOCTOR MAN!!!! *(Everyone stops, music stops.)* He is the devil! Praise GOD!!! *(Raises arms in the air dancing, after akward pause, music resumes.)* Come on Sisi — please! 121? Oh I know it, ya, I know it. Thanks Sisi — Thank you. *(Makes her way back through the pews.)* Excuse me, sorry, pamsoroi, sorry baby, pamsoroi...*(To congregation member.)* Ha? Oh, I am fine, I just felt the spirit telling me to go see a friend in need — but praise God, He is from where all blessings flow! *(Rushes out.)*

NINE: KEYSHA
(Short for Keyshawn)

MISS KEYSHA. *(To the waiter.)* No, the water is fine. But could you bring some lemon. And sugar. No, I don't want no lemonade. Did I ask for lemonade? If I wanted lemonade I would order lemonade. Thank you. *(To NIA.)* Okay. So, should you have his baby? Should you have his baby? Should a dope fiend in a crack house run from the police? Hell yeah, you should have his baby. *(To the waiter.)* Waiter! *(To NIA.)* No, I don't, Nia. I really don't see what the dilemma is. It's not like you got pregnant by some ole, dirty, jerry curl juicy, gold-tooth pimp. We talkin' Darnell Smith. Dar-nell Smith. The crem de la crem. Do you know how many girls pokin' needles in condoms tryin'ta have his baby. And here you sit, on the come-up like Mary pregnant with Jesus, talkin' 'bout should have his baby. Have Miss Keysha taught you nothin'? What else you gonna do? That's Darnell Smith's baby and everybody know Darnell Smith. And these recruiters is lickin' his anus tryin' to get him to go to they school. I'm talking UCLA, Notre Dam-a. Indian-I-A, all of 'em. And you know what's gonna happen when he get outta school. He goin' straight to the NBA. Do you know what that mean? Do you know what that mean? That mean you…we 'bout to be set for life. For LIFE. I'm talkin' Malibu mansion. Mercedes Benz. SL class on Sprewells! I'm talkin' Louis Vetton luggage…no, no, no. Real Louis Vetton luggage. VIP parties, backstage passes…hold on. *(He has an orgasm.)* Ooooo! I can't believe I gave him to you. He was right on the line, he coulda went either way, either way. I was the one introduced ya'll when you was eight cuz I was tired of you followin' me around. Uhh huh. Those were my dark days of darkness — before I became the fine specimen you see before you. We was all staying' wit Auntie Gina — all of us up in that one room; and her makin' me take you with me when I went out, knowin' you would tell if I did somethin' wrong. Why you think I'd have you to go play with Darnell? To get yo' nosey ass out my business. Who knew Darnell would end up a damn star? He about to be so rich. I shoulda went ahead and did him then, with his little eight year old pee pee. *(Acting out what that might look and sound like.)* Speakin' of pee-pee. I gotta go tinkle. *(Laughing, he EXITS.)*

   WITCHDOCTOR. *(Sings, and dances complete with fly whisk and headress.)* Mhondoro dzinomwa muna Save. Mhondoro dzinomwa muna Zambezi *(x2, Sits.)* Don't mind all this *(Indicating traditional attire.)* I had some whites, matourist, they wanted to see the witchdoctor like the one they see on TV. I didn't know I could do those dances, hey! *(Dances from a seated position a bit.)* But it was good, my daughter, I gave them a show, they give me some money, everyone was happy! But, the spirits are happy to see you my daughter. They were angry at you — because — you have been running to these other cultures for your answers; but now you have returned they are happy. But you must know that this is from where all answers flow. These are your roots. So what's the problem here, eh, don't say anything, the ancestors will speak it to me. *(Throws bones.)* Mmmm, you are a professional woman, very well dressed, what, what. I see you are married, ya. Not enough children, not enough children from you, yah. But you're hips are looking like you could have some more if you wanted. Don't tell me you are pregnant — I knew that, I was going to say it! Don't anger the ancestors. *(Whisks himself angrily with whisk. Throws bones, sniffs the air, rubs nose.)* I'm smelling fear, fear of the husband, fear of the husband, fear of the husband — but why? *(Silences her with his hand, throws bones again, looks at them, then at her.)* Why are you so sad, you are pregnant, but you are sad, scared, and sad, scared and sad — but you are pregnant — he doesn't know eh? Yah! But what are you scared of?... WHY are you telling me? You are going to bring on the wrath of the ancestors. *(Whisks himself with whisk.)*. So you are sick, ahh...its The Sickness? Okay, okay, okay, okay *(gathers bones)*, we don't cure that. No one can cure that. There was a time, we thought it was a joke, we would call it American Ideas for Discouraging Sex. But now, now ahh, what we have seen, we know better. But you can come back to me when the illnesses start, I can help you with those symptoms. You can bring your husband to me too, if you tell him, I have a couples' discount. *(Claps his hands.)* Hey! Stop crying! Usacheme mwanawangu! You think you are the only one dealing with this problem? If you go outside you can count, one, two, three — he has it. One, two, three — she has it. You are not special, there are many people who have this thing and still live their lives! As for the other problems I've seen here *(Indicating bones.)*, I can help you with those today. For the fear of your husband beating you or leaving you, there is a love potion, a muti. AH — it is very popular these days I am running low. Rub it on his penis thrice a day. He will never leave you or forsake you. DON'T ask the great ones how to do it! That is your concern. But, you women know how to get it when you want it, he he hehehehe. That one will allow the baby to die before it is born. That way it won't have to suffer. But don't confuse the two or your husband's penis will look like a piece of tree bark by morning. *(Winces continually at the though and whisks himself, Starts singing again.)* That is all. And don't be so afraid my daughter, you are not alone. *(Holds out hand while singing, gets cash looks, holds out hand again, looks satisfied. Keysha RE-ENTERS.)* Sharp. Be gone. *(Keeps singing.).*

KEYSHA. Where is the complimentary bread. I tell you, that waiter got three mo' minutes — *(To NIA.)* Stop lookin' so sad. You not dyin', the world ain't over. You ain't the first one to end up pregnant. You should be happy! 'Cuz, you rollin' in the game with the big dogs now WOOF, WOOF! But let me warn you: this is not high school — these girls will be after Darnell and these bitches is ruthless. Don't trust none of 'em. They would fuck yo' man and yo' daddy in the same day. I've seen it happen: sports will turn these men into fools, but it'll turn women into... — Halle Berry in 'Jungle Fever': *(Mocking)* "Can I suck yo' dick? No? Uh, can I suck *yo'* dick? Anybody dick? Everybody dick?" Just wait 'til he get a little money, a little more fame — I already see that nigga every weekend with his hand indiscriminately placed between somebody's legs. And them girls! Please! They love it. Well, they may cum, but they will go cuz they ain't shit to him. You got his baby. You stayin'. But it won't be easy. 'Cuz he'll be out with two, three of 'em at the same time every night and won't think nothin' of it. Then he'll bring you back some nastiness, his PR person will get involved and the next thing you know, you readin' about how you tried to give it to him to bribe him outta some money or somethin'. Hell yeah, we want to be paid and pampered, but not enough to be catchin' no STD. You remember my roommate Monica? Monica. You know, *(Imitates MONICA.)* Yeah her. *(With discretion.)* She had Chlamydia. Girl, yes! Walkin' around with it, thought it was a damn yeast infection. By the time she asked me to help her to the clinic, she couldn't even walk. And when she got there they said she had waited so long it turned into P-I-D — Pussy in Distress, yes. She got that shit from Jerry — that muthafucka didn't even know he had it. He coulda been walkin' around with herpes, shit, AIDS and not even know it. Of course she was afraid to tell him! I had to confront his punk ass and you know what he said? He said, "I don't know whatchu talkin' 'bout. That's on her," like she gave it to herself. That nigga was on the DL, had Chla-my-di-a and he was still tryin' to make it seem like it was all on her. Like she did it like all by herself. How you even do that? What, you be like *(She imitates what giving herself a sexually transmitted disease would look like.)* — Okay, okay, okay. The point is this: These men don't give a fuck about you. All you are to them is a piece of ass. And I'ma be damned if I'ma let my cousin get used up and then end up with nothin'. If you're givin' it up, then you best believe he givin' it up too. And you sho' ain't havin' no babies for free. That is not prostitution, that's called takin' care-a you. I mean, look-atcha mama! She dated some first class Negroes, had they baby, but still couldn't pay her rent. The last thing you wanna be is some hood-rat, baby-mama, walkin' around with cold sores and house shoes; buyin' government cheese with food stamps when yo' baby daddy in the N-B fuckin' A, and playin' husband to some other bitch and her kids. Then who the one lookin' stupid? Now, at least if you his wife, you get half, even if he divorce your ass; even if you do get Chlamydia. Then, whatever way it go, you won't never have to worry about money, and can do whatever the fuck you wanna do. Write your poetry, be Maya Angelou, whatever. Listen to me: Don't let that boy out your sight. Remind him that you was the one at his games before anybody knew his name. Tell his mama you carrying his baby. Mmm-hum. Naw, go 'head, make it a family affair. Didn't you say you met her at they family picnic? See! She probably already like you! And once you have her, it don't matter what he say. Don't stop 'til you get keys to the crib and a ring on that finger! Should you have his baby…how else you gon' pay me back for all the shit I did for you? Nia, havin' a baby is a blessing. I mean, think about it. I look better than all ya'll heifers put together, but I cannot have a baby out my ding-a-ling. Whatever you do, I'ma always be your cousin, but remember, we already live in hell. Don't make it so you have to spend eternity there too. God gave you that baby. That baby is yo' ticket out. *(He EXITS.)*

TEN: SEX WORKER

SEX WORKER. *(ENTERS smoking)*: Dahling, dahling, dahling. How the bloody hell am I supposed to know how to make a man fall asleep so you can put love potion on his penis? Don't believe those stories about us sexworkers stealing the penises of men who don't pay. That's all bullshit! *(Starts to sit, gets back up.)* Just give me a second my dahling, *(Takes out cloth tucked in side of pants, wipes between her legs.)* What a messy bastard….that's better. *(Sits)* Right, shit, you've got yourself into a pot of poo my girl! Who would have thought Miss Priss Abigail would get herself in such a bind! But, let me help you out my sister, since you have come to your old high school chum for advice. You have to face the truth. Your marriage is ova. You think you can make him stay? You know how these men are! He will blame you for everything, even though you got it from him. And the in laws!! Do you remember Elizabeth Chidzero? It happened to her! Sent back to her village, penniless, the kids taken by the bastard and his family, even though she got it from him! Now she is waking up to the cockrels singing "kokoriko" — dancing at those fucking village pungwes for those old farts, and she bathes in a filthy river, even though she's as sick as a bloody dog hey! You think it won't happen to you? You'll find yourself back in your village, grinding corn singing "dum dum duri, dum dum duri." Ha, and you were always the one who was going to go to America or something and become rich and famous. What did you say your man's name was again? AHHHH *(Deep in thought, then looks back at ABIGAIL.)* All I'll say is I am not suprised. Shame. The best thing I can offer you, my sister. Is a new lifestyle. Leave the bastard. Because he gave you Aids! I can hook you up with a nice beneficiary. Who will take such good care of you, my love, you will never need that man of your again. He will give you enough doughs to get the medicine and save that baby! You can take your son, get your own place — you take care of the man every now and then. BUT — you get the doughs, buy the drugs. And you will live so much longer futi. And no bullshit in law stress. What have you got to loose my dahling? I don't understand the prob- Ohh, ha! You think this lifestyle is planned or something? The economy is shit, my dear. In case you haven't noticed. I was a secretary, couldn't pay for my rent, couldn't pay for my electric, I couldn't pay for my fucking DSTV! And I was NOT going back to watching Dead BC. No offense. So I did it once, did it twice, next thing you know I had a business. Listen, there is NOTHING wrong with being a kept woman. It's the least these bastards can do for us. And it's a fair trade, almost like going back to the barter system. And these African men, they love to flex their dollars, makes their dicks hard. So, it's there for the taking. You have to decide what's more important to you. Remain Miss Priss Abigail, or become a survivor. Because, you can't save both your marriage and that baby. You can keep quiet about it, act as if nothing is wrong and die horribly — watching your kid die too, all because you wanted to remain the perfect little Shona, Zimbabwean wifey. Which many have done. Or you can take care of yourself and your children. Personally, I want to be a mother. I have this one guy; he's a client, but he's a really nice guy hey! He wants me to have his baby. He says, no condoms. Saka, me, I say, why not! It's important to be a mother, it's the one thing we can do that these bastards can't! This is just a hope for me, but you, you have children, so be a mother. And forget about that potion girlie Those n'angas are mad. If they had anything that worked Africa wouldn't even have Aids. *(Looks outside.)* Shit! Sorry dahling, it's another customer — and this one needs a little bit more time. He's one of those old government chef bastards. The machinery takes so much longer to oil. I can't even get into it. *(puts out cigarette)* Abi, Abigail — think about what I said, you have to do something, you can't keep running around like Speedy Gonzales! This is the best answer you are going to get! *(Straightens out wig and shirt, looks over at client approaching.)* Hi, howzit!?

(Adlibs and overlaps with the GAIL: "Hi, howzit...I'm fine,"
"Just don't be rough today, Chef!!".)

ELEVEN: GAIL

GAIL. Just be quiet, please! Shhh! Damn it, Darnell! I said to take your medication and use a condom. Use a condom. I told him to — You kids don't think. You don't think beyond your own little circle of existence. You think this is a video game? This is life. Real life. You don't get to start over! 'Cause he's just a boy, he's a baby, how is he supposed to know how to — when you all just keep tossin' yourselves at him! Don't give me that look. I see the way you look at him. Salavatin' with dollar signs in your eyes. You probably thought that if you latched onto him you could ride him all the way to the top. You think you the first one to try to lock him down? Ask his agent: he's already had two paternity claims. Sit down. Sit back down! Why should I have told you anything, Nia? This is a private family matter. You should have kept your legs closed. And I warned Darnell about ya'll. I said, "Darnell, baby, stay focused. You can't afford to get caught up." I made sure he played in all the right districts, with all the right coaches, he was seen by the recruiters! Look at his trophies. Look at them! Does this look like AIDS to you? Do you think he would be being recruited if anybody knew? Do you think he would be getting a scholarship? That's right! A scholarship for outstanding athletic achievement — to my son. So, no, nobody knows. It's none of they damn business. You consider what people will think about you if they knew. You think they gon' treat you the same? When you mention it, even the people you thought loved you will have you eatin' outta paper plates. Everybody turns on you; little kids say nasty things to you. Even the people at church! They gon' whisper behind your back; point at you in the pew, sayin', "That's what happens to people who sin with the devil." Think it won't happen. Now, I'm trying to help you, Nia, but you have got to promise me — Is this about money? Huh? Cuz I can get you money, Nia. Give me a couple of hours and I'll get you … $5,000. *(MAID ENTERS, singing, starts cleaning.)* How's that sound? That'll be enough to get you a place, have some money left over to do what you got to do. That's what we'll do: I'll get you $5,000 for now, and we can worry about later, later.

TWELVE: MAID

(MAID, on hands and knees, cleaning the floor, singing 'Tauya naye nemagumbezi'.)

MAID. Oh…Miss Abigail, masikati, maskwera sei? Ndaskwera. I have put out the chicken and samoosas for Simbi's party, and the man is here with the jumping castles, but he wants to know if you want the jumping castle, kana the jumping giraffe. And that crazy little friend of Simbi's Fungai Mparaza he had to come early — and he has already broken two plates Miss Abi! And Bhudi Gilbert called, he said he was coming with the braaai stand — MissAbi are you okay? My husband? I don't have a husband MissAbigail. No, ya, of course, my family wants me to have one but I don't want. Anyway my family now its just my brother and aunts and uncles. My mother and father — they died kuma 1998 and 1999, then my sister kuma 2001. They had a long illness. Anyway, me I said, it's better to be alone, love between a man and a woman seems to end in death around here. And people say stupid things to me, but I don't care. Oh, they say things like — 'eh, she thinks she is too good to get married, maybe she thinks she's a man. Eh, you don't want us — you are ugly anyway." *(Talks to imaginary men.)* I would like to say to them: YOU are ugly anyway and you probably have something then you will beat me and leave me to suffer when I get it from YOU!!! No thanks! But I just keep quiet. Saka, I am alone. I work here and go to night classes — I want to get a degree. Like you MissAbi, you work, you went to school, and you are a wife and a mother futi — I don't want that part but I admire that — then I know I can do it too zvangu. People say, you can't do anything without a husband in Zimbabwe – but I will try anyway. At least like this I can say, Ini I know who I am, where I am going — I know what I am working for. And I am moving *(gestures)* forward, forward, forward, not this way or that way but forward. Maybe I stand alone, but I know who I am — Mary Chigwada — not Mrs So and So with the in laws and brideprice, and going to his village to cook at the funerals chi chi — NO — just me Mary Chigwada. AHH, Miss Abi, — your mother and father are coming through the gate — ah, your mother looks so pretty! *(Straightening up.)* I am so glad you are back Miss Abi, there is so much to do, I haven't even put out the drinks yet and…Miss Abi — Miss Abi? Oh, maiwee! *(Rushes out.)*

THIRTEEN: THE PRAYER—BILLS, BILLS, BILLS

NIA. It smell like booty. I wish I could fly away. Dirty ass motel. Guess what, baby. Guess what? *(Dumping her purse.)* Today your mommy opened her purse to see how much money she had and she had a five dollar bill and a $5,000 check. $5,000. *(Folding up the check and putting it aside.)* But you know what? We don't need his money. No, we don't! 'Cause mommy will go tomorrow and see if they still want her at Nordstrom. What was they talkin' 'bout payin'? Five dollars. But no, baby, no, we can do it. We just got to budget. *(Tearing a piece of the five dollar bill with each item.)* See this, this right here is for my retirement fund. 'Cause Oprah says you should pay yourself first. This, this is for your college fund, 'cause you going to college. This is for rent…on our mansion in Malibu. And my Mercedes. What else? What else you want, baby? You can have anything you want. Oh wait! *(Tearing the last piece in three.)* Gas, water, and lights. What! That's the life right there, baby. You got, retirement, college, mansion, Mercedes, gas, water, lights. What! Ooooo! Mommy forgot to put food in the budget! How mommy forget to put food in the budget? But there's no more money. There's $5,000. *(She breaks down in tears.)* Because he knew. He knew. He knew the whole time — And he knows you're his baby cuz he the one made me pregnant. And now she thinks she can just throw $5,000 at me and I'ma just be quiet? $5,000 dollars. I sold myself for $5,000. Nope, baby, that's how much I cost. That's how much you cost. *(Balling up the check and throwing it down.)* No, no, we don't need his money. This is what we gonna do. *(Picking up the pieces of the five dollar bill.)* I'ma take the light money and make it the food money. Cuz we gotta eat. But we don't need no lights. *(A la "The Roof is on Fire".)* We don't need no lights let the muthafuckas burn! *(She b-boxes and makes a beat on the furniture.)* Come on, baby. Cuz we got, huh? What we got, huh? What we got?!? *(periodically breaking down and breaking rhythm)*

We got, we got Sunlight, Insight, Out of sight — out of mind.

Full-time, Lifetime
Out-of-time
I'm outta my mind
We gon' Re-define
Discipline
Undermine that bottom line
(Applying perfume.)
Drench myself in Vaseline
Make myself look feminine
I'll be dressed and drapped in Calvin Klein.
And he'll come home at dinnertime.
My womb is free of guilt and grime.
Before this change, before this crime.
Before the fall, before the climb (she begins to pray)
Please keep me from this constant grind
Help me see, although I'm blind
Help me breathe despite the slime
Help me live if you're inclined
Please don't decline my prayer.
I know it's nobody's fault but mine
I won't bitch, complain or whine
If you help me out, one more time
I will not let you down.
I'll give up sex, weed, and wine.
Everything. Everything.
Just plant my feet on solid ground.

(She sobs.) No. No! This what we gon' do. *(Picks up the check.)* Tomorrow we're going to go up to that scholarship ceremony. And I'm gonna make Darnell look me in the face and tell me I'm only worth $5,000. Then, I'm going to stand there

in front of all those recruiters, in front of the whole world and I'ma just say it. And then all the girls he been with's gon' know. And all the girls he was thinking about doin's gon' know. And then everybody will know. *(Balling the check up and throwing it down again.)* I'm worth more than this money. *(She begins to EXIT. She doubles back for the check.)* Tomorrow.

FOURTEEN: ABIGAL'S PRAYER

ABIGAIL. *(ENTERS, reading an old certificate.)* Huh, I won that thing! I won that thing! *(Reading)* This is to award Abigail Moyo of Malbereign Girls High as the winner of the National Interschools Public Speaking Championship, 1994, Harare, Zimbabwe. I won that thing. What was my speech again? Oh, oh! Of course! *(Steps up on bed.)* The New African Woman — Modernizing and Post Colonizing. I was once number three of four wives — yet I chose to rise. I was once denied usage of the same toilet as you *(laughs)* — I always had to look for a white — yet I chose to rise. In me is the blood of the great Mbuya Nehanda — the spiritual medium who fought and died for this land. In me is the pride of Winnie Mandela who marched the streets of Soweto singing 'Free Nelson Mandela' until they did. In me is the ferocity of the woman freedom fighter who let go of the milk of human kindness to fight for a free Zimbabwe! I am no longer the third of four wives, but the first of the first. And I can become whatever I please. Because my dreams can be a reality...*(She breaks.)* He knew, he knew, that bastard. *(Steps down.)*...how long...how long have you been bringing your hures into my house? Have you been sleeping with them in my Woolworths sheets from Joburg? But I knew it, I knew it all along, with the late nights and the way he was smelling…but what could I have done Baba? You are the one who said two become one, two flesh become one — and that's what I did — So how did you allow one flesh to rot into the other when I lived according to your word? And how can this be your plan for my life? You want me to die like a prostitute? That's your plan? That's what you have been building me up to? And don't give me that trial and tribulation bullshit! I have come too far, I have done everything the right way! What more did you want from me? You've got to help me Baba, you've got to help me, you've got to help — *(Stops, to catch her breath, goes silent, drops to her knees.)* Okay, okay, I will tell them. But this is what I ask: DON'T you let them blame me. You make them stand by me. And support me. And you make Stamford stay put. You make him still love me and take care of me. Because he's still mine and I am not giving up everything I worked for. And I want my baby, so don't you let it have this illness. *(Grips belly.)* You have to fight this baby with whatever you have. You just have to fight it okay. And if I must die — don't let me die like Sisi Stella who was convulsing in so much pain they had to strap her to a bed. And don't let me die like Sekuru Lovemore who was covered in so many sores they couldn't even show him at the funeral. And if I must die let my chil — *(Knock on the door — ABIGAIL starts, sits on chair and composes herself. Cheerily.)* Come in. *(ENTER SIMBI.)* Hello my big boy. Are you enjoying your party? You look so smart, is this the outfit daddy bought you? It's very nice…huh? They want to sing 'Happy Birthday' already. Okay, tell them I am coming — tell them Mummy spilt something on her dress and I have to change it. Okay…okay so you go ahead baby… Simbi, dzoka mwanawangu, dzoka. *(Calls him back.)* Unoziwa kuti mummy loves you? Okay, saka iti 'mummy loves me.'

Good boy. Ita futi, 'mummy loves me.' Good, okay, okay, you go ahead…mummy's coming.

FIFTEEN: THE END

ABIGAIL. *(Singing Watinti bafadzi with NIA — both clear stage of stools.)* Watinta wafadzi watinti mbogoto uzagofa x2 "Pamsoroi, Baba naAmai, nababamukuru, naBhudi Gilbert, navatete. Tafara, we are happy you have come to celebrate Simbi's seventh birthday with us. In our culture I know the family shares everything, and takes good, good care of one another. So I know I can share this with you and get your support. Stamford, I am telling you this here so we can find a harmony okay. Stamford, we have to go to the clinic tomorrow morning because I…you… you and therefore we have acquired the acquired immune deficiency syndrome virus HIV and I am pregnant."

NIA. "Good evening ladies and gentlemen. My name is Nia James, and I'm here to say that Darnell Smith gave me AIDS!" Then I'ma rip up the check. No, I can't say that…

ABIGAIL. No — that acquired acquired thing is stupid… No, no this is good, he can't beat me or throw me out with my parents and Bhudi Gilbert there at his son's birthday futi…

NIA. …no, it's the right thing. Everybody should know…

ABIGAIL. He will have to beg my forgiveness. "Okay, okay, I forgive you – but you can't cheat anymore" —

NIA. "He could be giving it to everybody. If I had know, I would have never" —

ABIGAIL. "Now we must plan ahead for us and the children."

NIA. "I'm not a hoe. Everybody has sex."

ABIGAIL. "Yes I forgive you — no, no — don't hit him Bhudi Gilbert."

NIA. "I didn't make this disease. I didn't give this to myself."

ABIGAIL. "I choose to stay with you but you must find the money for treatments,"

NIA. I should have protected myself, but he —

ABIGAIL. "Because you got us into this trouble. Okay!"

NIA. I just wanted him to...

(ABIGAIL and NIA face each other in a mirror, but remain in opposite worlds.)

ABIGAIL. "And you must look at me and see me, Abigail Moyo Murambe."

NIA. "There's no amount you can pay me to take this away."

ABIGAIL. "You must treat me like a wife you respect" —

NIA. "Naw, I don't want yo' apology!"

ABIGAIL. "Because I know who I am!"

NIA. "I'm changing the course of history!"

ABIGAIL. "And I am moving *(Gestures)* forward, forward, forward — not this way or that. Okay!"

NIA. That's fine.

ABIGAIL. That's good.

ABIGAIL/NIA. So help me God. Let's go.

ABIGAIL. Okay kids, go play on the jumping castle!

NIA. *(To herself.)* Damn, it's a lot of people...

ABIGAIL. *(Faces family.)* Pamsoroi Baba, naAmai na babamukuru, navatete naBhudiGilbert.

NIA. *(To herself.)* There he is...

ABIGAIL. Tafara, we are happy you have come to celebrate

Simbi's seventh birthday with us...eh...

NIA. *(To herself.)* Just say it...

ABIGAIL. In our culture, we...move forward, forward, forward...

NIA. *(To the crowd.)* Hey! I have...something I want to say...

ABIGAIL. No, no, I mean...with a family...eh...

NIA. *(To the crowd.)* My name is Nia James...

ABIGAIL. we share everything...

NIA. *(To the crowd.)* And I just came to say...

ABIGAIL. and that's why I know I can say what is happening between me...and Stamford...here...

ABIGAIL/NIA. Eh...eh...

*ABIGAIL. Stamford and I are having another baby!!!// Pururdza *(Ululates)* !!! Eh, suwa, tinofara!! Ha? Ya, that was the news, that was it! Another boy, ya, that's what I was saying Tete! Another boy ya! Well, you were saying Simbi is getting lonely! So it's time, ya, it's time. Sure ya. Maita! Tinofara... hehe.

*NIA. //Congratulations! Oooa, Oooa! Oooa, Oooa! Huh? No, no that's what I came to say. Congratulations. Yeah. His mom's probably real proud, huh?! Hey! Can I get tickets to the games? Just two tickets? One ticket? I'ma get me a ticket, watch! You crazy! Heeee...

(Both characters laugh in synchronicity into a blackout.)

END OF PLAY

SHONA/ZIMBABWE GLOSSARY

Aiwa — no

Amai — mother (also used as a sign of respect to a woman).

Amai naba vako nevese nemumhuri menyu —Your mother and father and your family

Beby — baby

Baba — father (also used to substitute as Lord, God.)

Babamukuru — older father (usually refers to an older uncle)

Bhudi — brother

Barance wemunhu — idiot of a person

Chef — a term used to describe men of power and influence in Zimbabwe

Chi chi — etcetera etcetera

Chisarai — Goodbye

Chisipiti — an affluent suburb of Harare

Commuter omnibus — A van used as a form of public

transport.

Dahling — darling

DSTV — equivalent of digital cable

Deddy — daddy

Dum dum duri — a song traditionally sung while grinding corn into flour with a large pestle and mortar

Dzoka mwana — come back child, come back

Edgars — Major clothing chain around Southern Africa

Ewe — you

Fotsek — An expletive originally used to address dogs.

Futi — again/also

Glen Lorne — An affluent suburb of Harare

Hartman House — one of the most affluent boys prep schools in Harare

Head boy — the top position a student can obtain in their final year of high school. A position of authority, from the British schooling system model, used in Zimbabwe as a result of colonization.

Heré — converts a statement into a question

Howzit — how is it going?

Ini — me

Ita futi — say again

Iti — say

Iwe waka pusa newewo uri HIV, futi Amai vako vane maronda panaapa — you are stupid and you have HIV, and your mother has sores here

Kana — or

Ka — a Zimbabwean exclamation — often used for emphasis

Kokoriko — Sound used to depict cockrels crowing

Kuma — in

Kumusha — a person's rural homeland

Kwete — no

Maita — thank you

Maiwee — an exclamation or expression of distress.

Masikati — Good afternoon

Maskwera sei — How are you?

Marara — bullshit/garbage

mati amaivangu vane AIDS — did you say my mother has AIDS

Mbuya Nehanda — legendary female Spiritual medium who stood up against the British when they first invaded Zimbabwe in the 1890s. They executed her.

mirai — wait

Mhondoro dzinomwa muna Save, Mhondoro dzinomwa munaZambezi — a song describing a lion drinking from the Save and Zambezi rivers.

Muboi — derogatory term that black people use to describe lower — classed black people

mwanawangu — my child

MunomuZimbabwe — here in Zimbabwe

Muri right — How are you (are you 'right')

ndibatsirewo — help me out

na — and

ndapota — please

ne — and

nhasi ririFriday — today is Friday

nodo — a children's game involving throwing a stone in the air and trying to move other stones out and inside of a circle while the stone is still in the air.

n'yanga — witchdoctor/traditional healer

Pamsoroi — excuse me

Pajero — prestigious Mitsubishi SUV in Zimbabwe

Paroadside — at the side of the road

Pururudza — A celebrative expression. Often termed as ululating.

Richiri jana rangu — Its still my turn

Sadza — a staple Zimbabwean starch dish made from cornmeal, often word used to reference food in general.

Saka — so

Saka wati Amai vangu vari HIV? — So you said my mother is HIV?

Saka hapana achatamba, hapana achatamba — So
    nobody is going to play, nobody is going to play.

SABC — South African Broadcasting Corporation

Sha — exclamation substituted for 'man' for example
    'come on man', 'come on sha.'   Also short for
    Shamwari

Shamwari — friend. Also used as an exclamation.

Sekuru — grandfather/older uncle

Sisi — sister

Suwa — sure

Tafara — We are happy

Tete — Aunt; specifically on one's father's side.

Tichaboona — See you

Totanga — let's start

Tinofara — we can all be happy
Tomato sauce — children's play song

Totamba chi — what should we play?

Truworths — Major clothing chain around Southern Africa

Unoziwa kuti — do you know that

Usacheme mwanawangu — don't cry my child

Vako ndivo vari HIV — They are the ones who have HIV

Vanhu vatema vanonetsa — black people are a pain

Village pungwe — traditional village meetings conducted in the rural areas

Watinta wafadzi wantinti mbogoto uzagofa — You strike a woman you strike a rock and you will die. (A South African song. Zulu- made famous by a musical production in the 1970s by the same name)

Wonai — look

Wuya — come here

ZBC — Zimbabwe Broadcasting Corporation ("Z" is pronounced "Zed")

Zimboes — a term used to describe Zimbabweans

Zvangu — myself — used as an emphasis

CAPTIVE
Jan Buttram

Comedy / 2m, 1f / Interior

A hilarious take on a father/daughter relationship, this off beat comedy combines foreign intrigue with down home philosophy. Sally Pound flees a bad marriage in New York and arrives at her parent's home in Texas hoping to borrow money from her brother to pay a debt to gangsters incurred by her husband. Her elderly parents are supposed to be vacationing in Israel, but she is greeted with a shotgun aimed by her irascible father who has been left home because of a minor car accident and is not at all happy to see her. When a news report indicates that Sally's mother may have been taken captive in the Middle East, Sally's hard-nosed brother insists that she keep father home until they receive definite word, and only then will he loan Sally the money. Sally fails to keep father in the dark, and he plans a rescue while she finds she is increasingly unable to skirt the painful truths of her life. The ornery father and his loveable but slightly-dysfunctional daughter come to a meeting of hearts and minds and solve both their problems.

OTHER TITLES AVAILABLE FROM SAMUEL FRENCH

COCKEYED
William Missouri Downs

Comedy / 3m, 1f / Unit Set

Phil, an average nice guy, is madly in love with the beautiful Sophia. The only problem is that she's unaware of his existence. He tries to introduce himself but she looks right through him. When Phil discovers Sophia has a glass eye, he thinks that might be the problem, but soon realizes that she really can't see him. Perhaps he is caught in a philosophical hyperspace or dualistic reality or perhaps beautiful women are just unaware of nice guys. Armed only with a B.A. in philosophy, Phil sets out to prove his existence and win Sophia's heart. This fast moving farce is the winner of the HotCity Theatre's GreenHouse New Play Festival. The St. Louis Post-Dispatch called Cockeyed a clever romantic comedy, Talkin' Broadway called it "hilarious," while Playback Magazine said that it was "fresh and invigorating."

Winner!
of the HotCity Theatre GreenHouse New Play Festival

"Rocking with laughter...hilarious...polished and engaging work draws heavily on the age-old conventions of farce: improbable situations, exaggerated characters, amazing coincidences, absurd misunderstandings, people hiding in closets and barely missing each other as they run in and out of doors...full of comic momentum as Cockeyed hurtles toward its conclusion."
–Talkin' Broadway

TAKE HER, SHE'S MINE

Phoebe and Henry Ephron

Comedy / 11m, 6f / Various Sets

Art Carney and Phyllis Thaxter played the Broadway roles of parents of two typical American girls enroute to college. The story is based on the wild and wooly experiences the authors had with their daughters, Nora Ephron and Delia Ephron, themselves now well known writers. The phases of a girl's life are cause for enjoyment except to fearful fathers. Through the first two years, the authors tell us, college girls are frightfully sophisticated about all departments of human life. Then they pass into the "liberal" period of causes and humanitarianism, and some into the intellectual lethargy of beatniksville. Finally, they start to think seriously of their lives as grown ups. It's an experience in growing up, as much for the parents as for the girls.

"A warming comedy. A delightful play about parents vs kids. It's loaded with laughs. It's going to be a smash hit."
– *New York Mirror*